ALL BLACKS

ALL BLACKS

Ron Palenski

Hodder Moa

National Library of New Zealand Cataloguing-in-Publication Data

Palenski, Ron.
All Blacks / Ron Palenski.
(Unique NZ)
ISBN 978-1-86971-110-8
1. All Blacks (Rugby team) 2. Rugby Union football—
New Zealand. I. Title. II. Series.
796.3330993—dc 22

A Hodder Moa Book
Published in 2007 by Hachette Livre NZ Ltd
4 Whetu Place, Mairangi Bay
Auckland, New Zealand

Designed and produced by Hachette Livre NZ Ltd
Printed by 1010 Printing International Ltd., China

Front cover: Hachette Livre NZ Ltd.
Back cover: Photosport

All photos Ron Palenski, except pages 61 and 84 (Photosport), 74 and 77 (Peter Bush).

To the memory of Tom Ellison, without whom . . .

About the Writer

Ron Palenski is one of New Zealand's most experienced and prolific sports writers. His many books include the lives of notable All Blacks Jeff Wilson, Graham Mourie and Dave Loveridge and Olympic gold medalist John Walker. He wrote *The Games*, the definitive work on New Zealanders at the Olympic and Commonwealth Games. He has updated the seminal works of Rod Chester and Neville McMillan, *Men In Black* and *The Encyclopedia of New Zealand Rugby*. His general rugby books have included *Our National Game*, marking 100 years of the New Zealand union, *The Jersey*, which marked the selection of 1000 All Blacks, *Century In Black*, which marked 100 years of New Zealand test rugby, and *All Blacks v Lions*. He designed and set up the New Zealand Sports Hall of Fame in Dunedin. He was made an Officer of the New Zealand Order of Merit in the New Year Honours in 2002.

Contents

Acknowledgements

The publishers wish to thank the following people and organisations for their assistance with this book: Ron Palenski, Bob Luxford, Marc Weakley, Photosport, the New Zealand Rugby Museum, the New Zealand Rugby Union.

Introduction

Set aside any national bias and view New Zealand as others may view it. On a global scale, New Zealand is a pinprick of islands down toward Antarctica, dwarfed to the west by the land mass of Australia and to the north and east by the vastness of the Pacific. New Zealand is small and a long way from anywhere.

Isolated and barely registering on any strategic Richter scale, New Zealand *is* known and has made an impression on the larger world in a manner that belies its size and geographical remoteness.

There are many reasons for that. In the modern world, the marketing of tourism is a considerable factor in exposing New Zealand to the world, and in exposing foreigners to the charms of New Zealand. Farm products from New Zealand have been on shopping lists in the northern hemisphere for more than a century.

A country's greatest resource, it has often been said, is its people. And New Zealand people have for more than a hundred years sloughed off the tyranny of distance to make their marks in the wider world. The deeds of some are well known but there are others about whom books and learned dissertations have been written yet they are barely known in the land of their birth. Ernest Rutherford, Katherine Mansfield, Janet Frame, Ed Hillary and Peter Jackson are just some of the prominent names with which New Zealanders are familiar. The name of Harold Williams, a linguist and Russian expert in the first quarter of the twentieth century, is one in the barely known category.

There is also the sporting elite who, many would argue, have done the most to bring the attention of the wider world to New Zealand. New Zealand's flag may not be instantly recognisable to non-New Zealanders and its national anthem has never attained the trans-national fame of the anthems of some countries. New Zealand's flag, like so many others, is red, white and blue, but black is the colour with which New Zealand is most associated. That is because of sport or, more specifically, because of rugby. Black and the Silver Fern. That is the unique livery New Zealand presents to the world — distinctive and instantly recognisable.

Practically every New Zealand sport followed rugby's lead and adopted black for its national team uniform; many also use the Silver Fern and many, in the modern mania for nicknames, use names that derive from the All Blacks.

It all started with a privately organised rugby tour of Britain and Australia in 1888–89 by a team designated the New Zealand Natives. It was supposed to have been all-Maori but some Pakeha (European) players were added. The Native name was retained in the mistaken belief that the supplementary Pakeha were all born in New Zealand. They weren't. But never mind, the Natives they remained. They wore black jerseys with a Silver Fern on the left breast. They also took the haka to Britain. One of them was Tamati Erihana, or Tom Ellison as he was better known. He was one of rugby's earliest thinkers and four years after the Natives' tour, he persuaded the newly formed New Zealand Rugby Football Union to adopt the black jersey and the Silver Fern as its own.

The next tour of Britain by a New Zealand rugby team, in 1905–06, established the colours in the consciousness of the world. They became the All Blacks and the national colours took hold. Even the national soccer and league teams were known for years afterwards as 'the All Blacks', soccer only becoming the All Whites during their 1981-82 World Cup campaign, and the league team the Kiwis after World War II.

The Original All Blacks also took the haka to Britain and gave the 'Ka Mate!' haka a wider fame — the haka with which the All Blacks are now most associated and which is rendered by all manner of people in all manner of circumstances around the world.

It is necessary to understand that the tour by the Original All Blacks was not merely seen in sporting terms, either by people in New Zealand or in Britain. In the imperialist flavour of the times, it was seen by New Zealanders as a way of showing

The forerunners of the All Black legacy — the 1905-06 Originals.

'the mother country' how well the 'son' had developed and how adept it had become at one of the most English of games. Similar attitudes were expressed in Australia in relation to its success with cricket.

There was no more fervent proponent of this view than the New Zealand Premier, Richard John Seddon, who saw the tour as a way of extolling the virtues of New Zealand, at the same time as demonstrating that the country was a worthy outpost of Empire. After the All Blacks beat Hartlepool clubs in the eighth match of the tour, Seddon told the London *Daily Mail*:

'The natural and healthy conditions of colonial life produce stalwart and athletic sons of whom New Zealand and the Empire are justly proud.'

New Zealand's Agent-General (a forerunner of High Commissioner) in London was William Pember Reeves, a man of many parts, one of which was playing rugby for Canterbury in his youth. He told the *Daily Mail* why New Zealanders were so good at rugby:

'The climate is a great factor . . . brisk, breezy and bracing . . . our country is peopled with a race inheriting the sporting instinct of British stock, with vaster opportunities . . .'

Eighteen years later, when the All Blacks toured Britain unbeaten in 28 games and earned themselves the nickname 'the Invincibles', Reeves waxed lyrical:

> So from two ends of an Empire met
> Stocks of the self-same brand.
> All Blacks, All Whites, they were twain, but yet
> Sons of one brave land.
> She'll laugh — "Good Lads!" when, as seasons turn,
> Our sons to their sons relate
> How the jersey black and the famous Fern
> Won through unto Twenty-Eight.

While other New Zealanders were achieving in their own ways, it was the All Blacks who gained the publicity and put New Zealand's name in the forefront. The value of sport, and rugby in this case, in gaining recognition for New Zealand has not changed. When the first Grand Slam All Blacks toured Britain in 1978, the High Commissioner in London, Sir Douglas Carter, followed the team whenever he could,

and at the end of the tour he was asked what the tour meant to him as a politician with no particular involvement in rugby: 'They're doing my job for me,' he replied.

The value of the All Blacks as a national drawcard was also clearly seen by the Prime Minister, Helen Clark, in 2005 when she readily changed her schedule to go to Dublin to help present New Zealand's case to stage the 2011 World Cup. Also there was the All Black captain of the time, Tana Umaga, and a former captain, Colin Meads. The three were portrayed in a cartoon, celebrating New Zealand's successful bid. All three were pictured in All Black jerseys.

The Cup's coming home: captains past and present Colin Meads and Tana Umaga, Prime Minister Helen Clark, NZRU chairman Jock Hobbs and chief executive Chris Moller reflect on a job well done after securing the hosting rights for the 2011 World Cup.

Key Dates

1870	First games of rugby in New Zealand
1888	New Zealand Native team tours Britain, Australia and New Zealand; performs haka before some matches
1892	New Zealand Rugby Football Union formed
1893	Black jersey with Silver Fern decided on for national team, but with white knickerbockers
1901	Black shorts introduced for first all-black uniform
1902	Ranfurly Shield introduced
1903	New Zealand play first test (against Australia in Sydney)
1904	First test (against Great Britain) at home
1905	New Zealand team tours Britain and is known as the All Blacks for the first time; performs 'Ka Mate!' haka before some matches; Wales respond with national anthem for the first time

1907	Four Original All Blacks join first New Zealand league team
1924	All Blacks in Britain and France perform haka written specially for them
1931	Bledisloe Cup presented for competition between New Zealand and Australia
1978	All Blacks complete Grand Slam tour of Great Britain and Ireland, beating all four 'Home Nations'
1987	All Blacks win first rugby World Cup
1995	Rugby drops amateurism regulations
1996	All Blacks win inaugural Tri Nations tournament for competition between New Zealand, Australia and South Africa

Why Rugby?

Of all the countries that field rugby teams, in very few is the game of any national, let alone international, significance. One of the criticisms of the rugby World Cup is that likely winners come from only four or five countries and in some of them, rugby is not the dominant sport.

Even in Australia, the only country to have won two of the first five World Cup tournaments, rugby competes against league, AFL and soccer for players, popular support and news media attention and it has never had an undisputed Number One billing.

Only in New Zealand, Wales and South Africa could rugby be said to have been, historically speaking, the dominant winter sport, and in South Africa that has to be qualified because of the years of white minority rule. Rugby was the white man's game.

In New Zealand, there has seldom been any doubt about which sport has dominated. Sometimes rugby's role in society has been questioned but its dominance has never been supplanted. Of course there is an element of cause and effect here — if rugby were not a widely followed, influential sport, there would be no point in commenting on its impact on society, for good or for ill.

In an international playing sense, New Zealand has also been dominant. Its record of 72 per cent success in test matches is easily the best. The next is South Africa with around 65 per cent. Only three other countries, France, Wales and England, are above 50 per cent. In all matches by the All Blacks, the success rate is in the mid-80s.

The All Blacks have historically been viewed almost in awe by opponents. 'There is something about the blackness of the All Black jersey that sends a shudder through your heart.' So said the great Welsh halfback, Gareth Edwards. Another fine British player, Scottish fullback Andy Irvine, once said he thought that Scotland would never be good enough to beat New Zealand. He's right so far. Of the other 'major' rugby countries, Ireland are also waiting on their first win against New Zealand. When the All Blacks are beaten in Britain, it is cause for prolonged celebration. Welsh clubs that have had wins over New Zealand still have regular reunions every year (though numbers are dwindling). Llanelli's win in 1972 was perpetuated in song; Munster's victory against the All Blacks in 1978 was recorded in a play, *Alone It Stands.* And still it does.

So how did all this come about? How and why did an isolated group of islands in the south of the South Pacific cotton on so well and so effectively to a game that had been developed largely by the upper middle class elite in southern England?

Sport, along with bibles, blankets and beads, was a part of the cultural baggage of the British Empire. Through the efforts of Arthur Swan, who was the New Zealand Rugby Union's official historian, the origins of the game in New Zealand can be pinned down specifically.

In the early years of European settlement, what football there was was a conglomeration of various forms of football that had gradually developed at English public (that is, private) schools or on the Australian goldfields. Schools such as Rugby and Westminster and Eton had their own games and their own rules and to these were added the rudimentary form of Australian rules that had been devised in Victoria (the game was first known as Victorian rules).

The evidence for the origins of rugby in New Zealand points squarely at a young man from Nelson, Charles John Monro who, as was the norm for sons of rich fathers in the nineteenth century, had been educated at Christ's College in Finchley in north London, a school that briefly adopted the football rules which applied at Rugby. Monro returned to Nelson in January of 1870 and a couple of months later watched his former Nelson College schoolmates playing their version of football. He persuaded them to adopt the Rugby rules. In a New Zealand sense at least, Rugby the school from then on became rugby the game.

The first rugby match in New Zealand, as proven by Swan, was played on 14 May 1870, at the Botanical Reserve in Nelson between teams of 18-a-side from Nelson College and the Nelson Football Club, which was known simply as the Town club. Monro played for the Town, the Nelson *Examiner* remarking in its report four days later: 'College played well and made a hard fight of it, determined not to give up, but at last a sudden rush by Monro and Clark decided the matter, the latter managing to kick a goal.'

Monro was far from the only rugby convert who brought the game to New

Zealand. Others also 'spread the word', but Monro was the first. A former pupil at Rugby, George Sale, was one of the pioneering figures at the University of Otago and he was a key figure in the gradual development of rugby there, quite separate from what happened in Nelson. Similarly, the Christchurch Football Club, which had been founded in 1863, transferred its allegiance to rugby in 1875 from its previous amalgam of association (soccer) and Victorian rules.

As an example of the nineteenth-century isolation between communities, rugby developed in Auckland in the early 1870s without its adherents being aware of what was happening in the South Island. Even more than 30 years later, when rugby was well established, the captain and vice-captain of the Original All Blacks, Dave Gallaher and Billy Stead, recorded in their magisterial *The Complete Rugby Footballer* that the first rugby match in New Zealand was in Auckland in 1872.

Monro, who later in life farmed near Palmerston North, was in no doubt about his place in rugby's history. In a letter to the editor of the *Dominion* newspaper in

A detail from artist Paul Wilding's impression of the first rugby match in New Zealand: Nelson College against Nelson Football Club in 1870.

Wellington in 1928, Monro wrote that his bringing rugby to New Zealand was a 'concurrence of circumstances'. His letter was prompted by a need for him to set the record straight after the newspaper had carried an interview eight days previously with one of his Town teammates in that first match, Richard Tennent.

Tennent had been the secretary of the Town club and, as an employer of the Bank of New South Wales, later played rugby in Wellington and Taranaki. In the interview, Tennent described the beginnings of rugby in Wellington when Monro organised a match at Petone between the Nelson club and a scratch side of Wellingtonians.

What annoyed Monro was that Tennent was described as the founder of rugby in New Zealand — but they were the *Dominion's* words, not Tennent's. Monro appeared not to notice that and he wrote: 'I have known Mr Tennent for more than 60 years and when we were young I knew him extremely well, upon the football field and in many other relations. He has always been a man of great energy and credit is due to him for the enthusiasm with which he entered into all forms of athletic sports, greatly to the advantage of the young men living in early times in my native town of Nelson.

'But when he states that he was the founder of rugby football in New Zealand he is not correct . . . Mr Tennent was simply a member of the Nelson Football Club, not one of whom had seen the rugby game, which they adopted at my instigation and played under my tutelage until familiar with the rules. I am not disposed to sit quietly down and allow my claim to be jumped by an old friend.'

Other than that letter, Monro in his later years was largely quiet about his pioneering role in rugby. He seldom attended matches, although he did travel to Wellington in 1930, at the age of 79, for the fourth test between the All Blacks and Great Britain. By then, New Zealand was firmly in rugby's grip. But why?

When the New Zealand union celebrated its seventy-fifth anniversary in 1967, the Chief

The man who brought rugby to New Zealand, Charles John Monro.

THE OFFICIAL PROGRAMME.

New Zealand
v.
Wales

CARDIFF ARMS PARK,
DECEMBER 16th, 1905.

Printed and Published by Rees' Electric Press, Plymouth Street, Cardiff,
in conjunction with the Welsh Football Union.

Justice, Sir Richard Wild — who had played for New Zealand Universities — was the keynote speaker at the anniversary dinner. He tried to sum up why New Zealand had embraced rugby like no other country.

'Rugby exactly suited our climate and our soil and it matches the temperament of the New Zealander and in large measure it has moulded the national character. It is the team element which provides a spur for the weaker spirit, a curb for the selfish and a discipline for all. It treats every man as an equal from whatever background he comes; there's no yielding to status in a tackle, there's no privilege in a scrum.'

The programme for the test match that quite possibly has been written and talked about more than any other.

When the first New Zealand team, the 1888 Natives, was in Britain, *The Times*, the voice of old Empire, tried to work out why rugby had taken hold in New Zealand and South Africa rather than soccer or, as it was called at the time, association football. 'The distribution of the association and rugby union games,' it said in an editorial, 'in our colonies is so contrary to what might have been expected that it must be set down either to chance or to the superior attractions of the rougher and more sweltering game.'

By the time the Original All Blacks were in Britain in 1905, New Zealand's Agent-General was William Pember Reeves, a writer, politician, poet and a former player for Canterbury. He wrote to the *Daily Mail* in general terms of the virtues of New Zealand and New Zealanders — plentiful food, ample leisure and universal education — and then in specific terms about rugby players: 'These clear-witted intelligent people are apt to use their brains as well as their muscles . . . there is nothing mystical about our team's success. They play with both ends . . . their heads and their feet.' He might have added that their hands were also quite useful.

The Myth of Webb Ellis

Myths are insidious little beasts. They worm their way into the subconscious and get handed down from generation to generation and become accepted and unchallenged as a fact of life. They are not outright lies; more mistaken beliefs, but the more they are repeated, the more the belief becomes ingrained. Sometimes when it's possible to expose a myth for what it really is, there are people who are much more comfortable with the myth because the myth is what they want to believe. The myth may bolster a country's ego and bolster its cultural baggage or it may reflect better on a person or group of people than the truth.

Myths abound in sport because people want to believe them or, just as likely, no one ever bothers to check them out. It's usually up to trained historians to demythologise stories from the past, but very few of them, relatively speaking, specialise in sport. An increasing number in recent years have explored the past of sport, but the proportion of them is not great compared with those whose specialties lie in other areas.

Rugby has its share of myths. It's actually founded on one: the story that an Anglo-Irish schoolboy, William Webb Ellis, in a eureka-like moment 'who with a fine disregard for the rules of football as played in his time first took the ball in his arms and ran with it', or so a plaque at Rugby School in Warwickshire says. So ingrained has that myth become that rugby's premier international prize, the World Cup, is formally known as the Webb Ellis Cup (and not, as some would have it, the William Webb Ellis Cup — another myth. But the Australians just call it 'Bill' anyway).

The guardian of the game, the International Rugby Board, even inducted Ellis into its International Rugby Hall of Fame in 2006. Let's assume for just a second that Ellis did what he was purported to have done and really did begin rugby. If so, he cheated according to the rules of the game he was playing. His induction into

the Hall of Fame must bring anticipatory excitement to all the other cheats rugby has known over the years.

There's no evidence that Ellis had anything to do with how rugby developed as a separate game from the various versions of football which were played in nineteenth-century Britain and had been played for centuries before. The first public information of Ellis's supposed deed came 53 years after the event, in 1876, when a former pupil of Rugby, Matthew Bloxam — who was not a pupil at the same time as Ellis — wrote to the school magazine, *The Meteor*, saying he had learned from

A sketch of William Webb Ellis from the *Illustrated London News*. This is the only known likeness of the subject of the myth.

an unidentified source that the change from a kicking to a handling game at Rugby 'originated with a Town boy . . . of the name of Ellis, William Webb Ellis.' Bloxam elaborated in another letter in 1880: 'A boy of the name Ellis . . . whilst playing Bigside at football in that half-year [1823] caught the ball in his arms. This being so, according to the then rules, he ought to have retired back as far as he pleased, without parting with the ball, for the combatants on the opposite side could only advance to the spot where he had caught the ball, and were unable to rush forward till he had either punted it or had placed it for someone else to kick, for it was by means of those placed kicks that most of the goals were in those days kicked, but the moment the ball touched the ground the opposite side might rush on. Ellis, for the first time, disregarded this rule, and on catching the ball, instead of retiring backwards, rushed forwards with the ball in his hands towards the opposite goal . . . '

Ellis died in 1872, four years before Bloxam's first letter. Bloxam had also died when the Old Rugbyeian Society decided to investigate the validity of the story. It concluded — surprise, surprise — that Ellis had indeed begun the distinctive game and the (English) Rugby Football Union latched on to its conclusion. It's relevant that at the time, English rugby was split between the south and the amateur ethic on the one hand, and the north, where clubs wanted players to receive compensation for lost time at work while playing, on the other. A majority of the northern clubs broke away to form what eventually became known as rugby league and the RFU readily accepted the Ellis myth so it could establish its version of rugby as the one true game. Interestingly, the RFU has since backed off from this view. Most historians since then have debunked the Ellis myth, citing an almost total absence of supporting evidence apart from Bloxam's two letters. Ellis himself died in obscurity in the south of France and again, there's no evidence to indicate he had any idea of the claims made in his name.

Ellis went to Oxford University in 1826 where he studied divinity (and played cricket for Brasenose College). He became chaplain of St George's, Albemarle Street, London and then rector of St Clement Danes in The Strand in central London. He was later rector of Laver Magdalene in Essex. Ellis evidently developed tuberculosis and moved to the drier climate of the south of France in an attempt to recover. He died in Menton on the French Riviera and was buried in the Vieux Château cemetery. His rugby fame subsequently caught up with him and his grave was 'discovered' by English sports nut and statistician Ross McWhirter in 1958. McWhirter, who was killed by the IRA in 1975, and his brother Norris founded the *Guinness Book of Records*.

The grave was subsequently repaired and a plaque attached which repeated the myth about his running with the ball and so beginning rugby. The grave continues to be tended by French and English enthusiasts and even, from time to time, by New Zealanders who know Ellis is but a footnote to rugby's history. The All Blacks stayed in Toulon along the coast from Menton in 1995 and television commentator Keith Quinn, director Gavin Service, photographer Andrew Cornaga and I made the 'pilgrimage', though with

Obscure in life, but remembered in death: the well-tended grave of William Webb Ellis in Menton in southern France.

no disrespect to Ellis, the trip doubled as a visit to Villa Isola Bella, the house in which Katherine Mansfield briefly worked while she too was searching for an end to her tuberculosis. But we found Ellis's grave and dutifully brushed off an accumulation of leaves and moss and had obligatory photographs taken.

Whatever Ellis did or did not do, it had nothing to do with the evolution of separate codes from the ancient forms of football that had been played in various parts of the world for centuries. English public schools played their own versions of football (such as Bigside at Rugby) and the gradual emergence of the two primary football codes, rugby and soccer, came over the issue of 'hacking', or kicking a player in the shins. The founders of what became soccer banned the practice before rugby did and they formed association football, while the others continued to play what became known as rugby union football. A further distinction between the two, late in the nineteenth century, was the acceptance of professionalism by association football, while rugby (especially after the northern split) was obsessively amateur.

The word 'soccer' incidentally, derives from the divergence of codes. Rugby adherents called their game 'rugger' for short and the association adherents followed with 'soccer' (from 'assoc'). The story goes that one Charles Wreford Brown, of

Corinthians and England, was having breakfast in his college hall as an undergraduate at Oxford. He was approached by a friend: 'Wreford, come and have a game of rugger after brekker.' 'No thank you John,' Brown supposedly replied, 'I'm going to play soccer.' The kicking game that grew out of common football formed itself into Association Football and was known for a time as 'Assoc', hence Brown's 'soccer' in preference to rugger.

Football is thus a generic name and it was only in the twentieth century that soccer became widely known as football while, confusingly, adherents of other branches of the same sporting family (Australian rules and American football) continue to know their games simply as football. Soccer adherents swear their game is the original and that rugby developed from it, but the reality is that both rugby and soccer at around the same time evolved from the various forms of football played in English schools and villages.

A few years ago, in another book, I outlined the Ellis mythology and that most revered of New Zealand rugby reporters, Terry McLean, phoned me and told me in his inimitable way: 'Ronnie my boy, don't destroy myths. We all need 'em.'

New Zealand rugby had its own myth for nigh on a century and it still lingers. The myth centres on how the New Zealand rugby team came to be called All Blacks.

The most popular story was one attributed to the longest-lived of the Original All Blacks, Billy Wallace. His view was that the name came about because a reporter on the London-based newspaper, the *Daily Mail*, referred to the team as 'all backs' because of the manner in which they played, that is, the forwards handling and running as much as the backs. Some sub-editor or linotype operator or other intervening hand thought the reporter mistaken and inserted an 'l' in the second word, thus making them All Blacks and establishing rugby's best-known team nickname. Wallace's recollection was that this came after the match against Hartlepool, the eighth of the tour. This was not just oral history. Wallace also wrote it down.

Writing about the Hartlepool match in his reminiscences which were published in the *New Zealand Sportsman* in 1932, Wallace said: 'Again the critics had to change their opinions and we were dubbed "the terrible All Blacks" by the *Daily Mail*.' Wallace added later on in his reminiscences: 'The name All Blacks had now stuck to us. It is the name with which we were christened by the *Daily Mail* and it caught on with the general public, though quite a number were misled into thinking we were a team of black fellows.'

But — and it's an important but — Wallace was wrong. The *Daily Mail* did not dub the team the All Blacks. It certainly called them that after the Hartlepool game, but the term did not originate with that paper or with its reporter, John Buttery, who covered most of the Originals' games. He was not in Exeter for their opening match, however, and it was after that the new name was first used publicly.

New Zealand beat Devon in Exeter by 55 points to 4. The next morning, a local newspaper, the *Express and Echo,* recorded: 'The visiting team were the first to make their appearance, and, as they filed onto the ground, they received an enthusiastic ovation. The All Blacks, as they are styled by reason of their sable and unrelieved costume, were under the guidance of their captain (Mr Gallaher) and their fine physiques favourably impressed the spectators.'

By the wording, it seems clear the team was known as the All Blacks already and that the *Express and Echo* just picked up on it. But the name had not been published in Britain until then and the team was certainly not known in New Zealand as the All Blacks at that time.

The *Daily Mail* and the Hartlepool match still figured in the naming story, but were only the second cab off the rank. The night of the team's 63–0 win against Hartlepool, the *Northern Daily Mail*, Football Edition — a sort of Saturday night sports special

— used the phrase. Its report of the match went on for 14 paragraphs before this introduction to a listing of the players' vital statistics: 'A glance at the undermentioned weights of the invincible 'all blacks' will convey some idea of the calibre of the team . . .' The name did not recur in the paper's coverage, which filled two pages.

The *Northern Daily Mail*'s parent paper, the *Daily Mail,* next took up the name. Its report recorded the score in the second paragraph and continued: 'This is a record in the tour, which is yet barely a month old, exceeding as it does by eight points the 55 points the "All Blacks," as the Colonials are dubbed, piled up against Devon.'

The next paper to use the name was the Gloucester *Citizen* a week later and 'All Blacks' first appeared in a heading in the *Daily Mail* on 19 October in its report of the Gloucester match. The next national newspaper to use the name was the *Daily Mirror*, on 6 November, and it gained common usage after that.

Buttery himself seems to contradict the 'all backs' theory because in his book about the tour, *Why the All Blacks Triumphed,* he wrote: 'The visit of the All Blacks

The *New Zealand Graphic* captioned this photo from the Originals' opening game against Devon: 'The Colonial backs start one of their dashing passing runs.'

— so dubbed because of their sombre football garb — has given a decided fillip to the rugby game.'

The name seems to have naturally evolved from a practice late in the nineteenth century to refer to teams by their jersey colours. For example, the first official New Zealand team in 1893 played against a team of combined southern North Island unions. The combined team players wore a variety of jerseys but mostly red and a newspaper report recorded a try by centre 'Tabby' Wynyard: 'Wynyard . . . with a determined effort got through the Red backs.' Similarly, the Wellington Rugby Football Union *Annual* — roughly equivalent to today's annual reports — referred to the New Zealand team as 'the Blacks'.

The manager of the Originals, George Dixon, kept a diary throughout the tour and on board ship on the way to Britain and he sometimes referred to the team as 'the Blacks'.

There was some truth to the 'all backs' theory, but the opposite of what Wallace later recalled. The Originals' vice-captain, Billy Stead, wrote a regular newspaper column throughout the tour for the *Southland Times*. Around the time of the team's first test, against Scotland, he reflected on the tour to that point and said how British writers were trying to work out why the team was so good.

'The nearest guess to the secret of our success,' he wrote, 'was by a well known army officer who suggested the altering of the name All Blacks to "all backs". For, he said, the moment the ball is secured or lost in the scrum then the whole fifteen 'sweeps' seem to be backs.'

Stead did not name the army officer but two were regular writers about the tour. One was Captain the Hon Southwell FitzGerald, who wrote for *The Sporting Life*, and the other was Major Philip Trevor, who wrote for *The Sportsman*. No record can be found of either of them referring to the team

The best-selling book produced by the *Daily Mail* after the Originals tour.

as 'all backs' but the phrase was used in a *Daily Chronicle* report of the Originals' 47–0 victory against Oxford University. The unidentified writer looked ahead to the next match, which was against Cambridge University, and wrote: 'I see that Cambridge are to employ the device of five threequarters and seven forwards in tomorrow's match and this seems to be a move in the right direction for the scrummage is the merest detail in New Zealand football. At the same time, even five threequarters, plus the two halves, cannot be regarded as possessed of the capacity to cope with a team who, ignoring all the traditional theories, convert themselves into all backs.'

There was yet another theory about the naming of the team, but again there was a want of evidence. This story says that when the team arrived in Taunton for the match against Somerset — the eleventh of the tour and therefore after Hartlepool — the players were greeted with newspaper billboards welcoming the All Blacks. Buttery supposedly made inquiries and told the team management a printer had in error inserted an 'l'. By this time, Buttery of course had used the All Blacks phrase himself.

For all the proof that the Exeter paper was the first to use the name All Blacks after the first game of the tour, and correctly identified the team's uniform as the reason for the nickname, the unproven stories still find a wide currency.

Black from the Start

Why black? It's a common question but it appears not to have an answer.

Some of the facts about why the New Zealand rugby team wears black are well known and indisputable. The first New Zealand rugby team to go to Britain was a team styled the New Zealand Natives in 1888–89. It was a privately organised venture and the team was called the Natives because originally, it was intended that all the players be Maori — a sort of New Zealand version of the Australian Aboriginal cricket tour of England 20 years earlier. But the complement was bolstered by four Pakeha (European) players, and organiser Tom Eyton reasoned they were born in New Zealand so the team could still be called 'Natives'.

It transpired that of the additions, Edward (Mac) McCausland had been born in Victoria and Pat Keogh in Birmingham, so Native it wasn't. But no one seemed to mind, certainly not British newspapers which referred to the team as 'the Maoris' anyway.

The significance of this private tour should not be overlooked in the history of New Zealand rugby. Historian Greg Ryan indicated his regard for it when he called his book about the tour, *Forerunners of the All Blacks*. They were. Not only did they establish a touring pattern that was followed for much of the twentieth century (though no official New Zealand team went even close to matching the Natives' 107 games in Britain, Australia and New Zealand), they also wore black.

The team's jersey was black with a silver fern on the left breast, in contrast to an earlier, also unofficial, New Zealand team in 1884 that wore a blue jersey with a gold fernleaf. (That team was managed by an Otago rugby identity, Sam Sleigh, and the blue mirrored that of his club, Dunedin, and province).

A photo taken in Queensland of most of the Native team. The flag on the left is New Zealand's first flag, known as 'the Flag of the Independent Tribes', which was approved in 1834, and the national flag, until it was superseded by the Union Jack in 1840.

Ryan and others record the details of the Native team's jersey, but not how the colour was arrived at. It could be that the answer is prosaic. Eyton, who was born in Britain, would have known that the British countries played in white, navy blue, scarlet and emerald green and it would have made no sense for his team to adopt any of those colours. Another simple reason could be that the range of colours available in imported bolts of cloth in the 1880s would not have been great. So black it was.

One of the star players of the Natives' tour was a remarkable young man, Tom Ellison, who had learnt his rugby at Otakou, colloquially known as 'the Kaik', near the entrance to Otago Harbour. 'I shall never forget my first game of football,' he wrote. 'It took place at the Kaik, Otago Heads, about the year 1881. I had heard a little about the game, owing to cousin Jack Taiaroa, the famous and unsurpassed Otago back, being a reputed champion at it, but I had not seen the game played or the rules of the game when a brother of Jack's brought down the first football that

One of the Native team's caps.

was ever seen at the Kaik. As soon as we set eyes on it, we were all there for a game, and immediately started on that poor, unprotected ball (which, by the way, consisted of the bladder only). What our main object was I cannot say, but mine was to see more of that ball and to know more about football . . . '

He certainly achieved the second of his ambitions. Eyton, in his book about the Natives' tour, said of Ellison: 'When on tour, he played as a forward and was second to none other in the Native Team. His knowledge of the finer points of the game; his weight, strength and activity rendered his services invaluable.'

The memorial headstone over Tom Ellison's grave at Otakou on the Otago Peninsula.

Fifteen of New Zealand
Versus
Wellington.

PETONE, WEDNESDAY, JUNE 21st, 1893.

A Novel Competition!
£10 GIVEN AWAY.

Every Purchaser to the value of 2s in Tobacconist's Goods, including Tobacco, can compete. Remember—Full value for your money. Full particulars obtained at

. WILLIAM PIPER'S
Empire Cigar Divan, Manners Street.

Evening Post Print.

Ellison had moved from Otago to be educated at Te Aute College in Hawke's Bay and from there on to Wellington, where he played for Poneke and was reputed to have been one of the prime movers in the development of the wing forward, the most distinguishing feature of New Zealand rugby until it was abolished in 1930. He was one of Wellington's two delegates to the first annual meeting of the New Zealand union in 1893 and he successfully moved 'that the New Zealand Representative colours should be Black Jersey with Silver Fernleaf, Black Cap with Silver Monogram, White Knickerbockers and Black Stockings.'

The programme for the first match by a New Zealand team under the auspices of the New Zealand Rugby Football Union.

No evidence has come to light, but it is assumed that Ellison chose the black with the silver fern because that had been the uniform of the Natives team. Two months after the meeting, the union dispatched its first team to Australia and, appropriately, Ellison was its captain.

There's no record of Ellison knowing, but the colours he favoured had already been claimed by the Feilding club in Manawatu, which had been founded in 1878. The club promptly gave New Zealand the priority. 'The original uniform of the Feilding Football Club was a black jersey with a silver fern,' the club's history records. 'We kept this for two or three years [more than that] until the NZRU decided that this would be a suitable jersey for the All Blacks. Consequently we had to make a change . . . '

The 1893 team's white knickerbockers came to just below the knees; the black jerseys had leather yokes and the caps had the letters 'NZ' interlaced on the front panels with the year, 1893, embroidered on the peaks. The next few teams had substantially the same uniforms but by 1901, the all-black strip first appeared, the white knickerbockers replaced by black shorts. There's no record of why the change was made.

Aside from changes in fashion and material, the All Blacks' uniform has been much the same since. Some traditionalists argued against the dumping of the white collar when adidas took over as apparel sponsor in 1999, but none of the early All Black jerseys had white collars.

The All Blacks wore white jerseys for the first time in 1930 when they played Great Britain, who wore blue, then changed again when Scotland first toured New Zealand in 1975. They continue to wear white against Scotland in New Zealand and sometimes when they play them in World Cups.

The All Blacks wear white for the first time. This is against Great Britain in 1930.

An Original Suggestion

A noted rugby administrator, Norman McKenzie, once suggested that the name 'All Blacks' should be reserved in perpetuity for the Originals, the team of 1905–06 that first gained the name.

McKenzie made his suggestion in the weekly newspaper, the *New Zealand Free Lance*, on the eve of the first test in 1959 against the British Isles.

'I have always regarded the title "All Blacks" as something that should be reserved solely to that band of pioneers who blazed the trail in the Homeland in 1905–06 and were described as such, by reason of their sombre uniform, by the English Press.

'Twenty-seven strong, 13 backs, 14 forwards, including two sick men for a start. Not for them a hint of replacements, and not a whisper of Craven's cramp or such like. They were tough and rugged warriors 54 years ago and a grand

advertisement for the colony of New Zealand as it was then.' (McKenzie's reference to Craven's cramp seems to be about the manager of the 1956 South Africans, Danie Craven, habitually dismissing injuries as cramp).

Rather than call all national teams the All Blacks, McKenzie preferred each team to be known simply as a New Zealand XV.

'. . . the thought arises that the NZRFU should, for the future, take pains to announce subsequent selections as the New Zealand XV,' he wrote. 'No one imagines that it is the best but it is the New

Norman McKenzie, the man who wanted the name 'All Blacks' kept just for the Originals.

Zealand XV to play the visiting international XV whichever country it comes from. In the Four Home Unions they are most precise in this respect and we should be the same.'

McKenzie spoke with authority. He was a member of the noted Wairarapa family that gave remarkable service to New Zealand rugby for the first half of the twentieth century. He coached the celebrated Hawke's Bay teams of the 1920s, had two separate terms as a New Zealand selector and managed the All Blacks in Australia in 1947. One brother, Bill, was an All Black; another, Ted, was a test referee and New Zealand selector; and another, Bert, was also a test referee.

McKenzie's idea of 'retiring' the name All Blacks with the Originals was a plan partly followed by the Australian Rugby League. It decided its national team would be called the Kangaroos only when touring Britain. It changed its mind in 1994, however, and decreed the team could be called the Kangaroos when they played in New Zealand as well. Now, they're called that whenever and wherever they play.

Followers of Fashion

The Original All Blacks and their uniform of black with a silver fern gave the nation its sporting colours and spawned a range of nicknames.

Such was the impact of the All Blacks that little thought seemed to be given to national teams in other sports wearing anything but black with a silver fern. The early Olympians, in 1908 and 1912, combined with Australia in Australasian teams and wore uniforms that were predominantly green. When the first purely New Zealand Olympic team was chosen in 1920, however, its colours matched those of the All Blacks.

So too did the first league team in 1908 which included four members of the Originals, among whom was wing George Smith, one of the organisers. That first team became known as the All Golds — a name coined in Sydney and reflecting perjoratively on their being professionals. Subsequent league teams were known formally as the All Blacks until 1938, when the name Kiwis, first used unofficially in 1921, finally stuck. The team had had a kiwi on the jerseys since before World War I.

Rugby also had its Kiwis — the Second New Zealand Expeditionary Force team — formed in Britain at the end of World War II and which helped re-establish international rugby in Britain. Its name was a natural progression from a range of wartime army-related organisations that used the name Kiwis, most famously the Kiwi Concert Party.

A New Zealand team played in the Australasian football championship — Australian rules — in Melbourne in 1908 and its players too wore an all-black uniform with a silver fern on the jersey (or guernsey, as they say in the AFL).

Interestingly, New Zealand, Australia and South Africa are among the few countries whose national sporting colours do not reflect colours in their national flags. Australia's green and gold — green for gum trees and gold for wattle — was first used for the national cricket team and other sports gradually followed. The Australian

FRANCE
c/
NEW ZELAND ARMY
1946

Government declared green and gold the official national colours in 1994, yet its flag, like New Zealand's, consists of only red, white and blue. The South African Rugby Board decided on green and gold for its team's jerseys in 1906 and a year later decided to make the springbok and the colours available to all South African sports teams.

Journalists had a hand in either originating or perpetuating each of the early sporting nicknames. All Blacks may not have been coined by a journalist but once taken up by them in Britain, the name stuck. Similarly, the league team was called Kiwis by a journalist, and later formally adopted by the New Zealand Rugby League.

The next most enduring national team name, the All Whites for the national soccer team, also came from a fertile journalistic brain when the team wore white while competing in the World Cup qualifying matches in 1981. For much of its previous history, the team had been known as the soccer All Blacks. The name Baby Blacks, for the largely new All Black team that played France in 1986, also came from a journalist. (All Blacks who had been in South Africa with the rebel Cavaliers team were declared ineligible for the French match when they got home and suspended for the next, against Australia).

The Kiwis — the 2nd New Zealand Expeditionary Force army team before the match against France.

Nicknames became of two types. Either they evolved naturally because of some distinguishing characteristic such as colour, or they were contrived. (The South Sydney league team, for example, is called the Rabbitohs because some of its original followers in 1908 sold rabbits at inner Sydney markets). The more recent nicknames in New Zealand fall into the contrived category. They became imposed for marketing reasons and most of them were derivative in some form or other of the All Blacks.

Through the 1990s there was a plethora of newly nicknamed teams, prominent among them the cricket team as the Black Caps after they had a brief period as the Young Guns (or, inevitably, Pop Guns when they failed).

One sport, softball, even adopted names without much regard for the history of its own parent sport of baseball. The national men's team came to be known as the Black Sox and the women as the White Sox. When the Chicago White Sox threw the World Series in 1919, they became known derisively as the Black Sox.

The nadir in the instant nickname market came in 2005 when the badminton team briefly flirted with the name of Black Cocks (combining one common derivative and the other of the shuttlecock used in the game).

Some of the sporting team nicknames which pay homage to the All Blacks:

All Whites	soccer
Black Caps	cricket
Black Ferns	women's rugby
Black Sox	softball
Black Sticks	both men and women's hockey
Ice Blacks	ice hockey
Kiwi Ferns	women's league
Max Blacks	cricket max (briefly)
Silver Ferns	netball
Tall Blacks	basketball
Tall Ferns	women's basketball
Wheel Blacks	Paralympics rugby
White Ferns	women's cricket
White Sox	women's softball

A Tall Black in action — New Zealand basketball
centre Tony Rampton.

Fame in the Name

The Original All Blacks had barely got their land legs back after they arrived home in March 1906 before enterprising business people tried to cash in on the new nickname.

They arrived back on 6 March and four days later the first company registered a trademark bearing their name. L. D. Nathan — a predecessor company of the long-running All Blacks' sponsor, Lion Nathan — sent off to the Patents Office a label for a new whisky. It read: '"All Black", the Very Finest Scotch Whisky, Imported and Bottled by L. D. Nathan and Co Ltd, Auckland.' (Pictured opposite.)

Twelve days later, the *New Zealand Gazette* recorded another application. It was lodged by a New Plymouth footwear company, Egmont Boot and Shoe Company, and its trademark had the words 'All Black' and 'Invincible' within the shape of a football. The company said it would apply the name to its boots and shoes. Its use of the word 'invincible' as applying to the All Blacks was remarkably prescient. The Originals' successors, the 1924-25 team, came to be known as the Invincibles after they went one better than the Originals and won each of their matches.

Another company lodged an application on 11 April, barely a month after the team's return home, and this one went the whole hog. It pictured a black-clad figure running with a ball under the right arm, and the words 'All Blacks' underneath.

It was the work of a Palmerston North tea packer, Goldingham and Beckett, and the trademark gave it the right to market an All Blacks brand of tea.

Black Gold

For most of its existence since its debut in 1905, the name 'All Blacks' was purely an unofficial nickname. It was a term widely used in the news media and by the public, and players were known as the All Blacks or as former All Blacks, but the New Zealand Rugby Football Union gave the name no official status.

When the union dispatched a team to Argentina in 1976 made up of players who had not toured South Africa earlier that year, the chairman of the union, Ces Blazey, was asked if the team for Argentina would still be known as the All Blacks. His reply was almost brusque. That name had no standing and was merely a phrase used by journalists, he said. 'It is officially a New Zealand representative rugby team.'

But times change. As rugby's commercial world widened, it quickly became apparent the best-known nickname in the game could become a money-spinner.

In 1986, at the urging of its marketing adviser, former All Black Andy Haden, the union adopted a stylised silver fern emblem and had it formally registered. A year later, the phrase 'New Zealand All Blacks' was also registered, the union ignoring complaints that it was a tautological phrase.

The protection of the name and of the stylised fern allowed the union to enter licensing arrangements with commercial companies such as suppliers and souvenir makers, and also gave them the legal stick with which to ward off potential ambushers.

Not content with one nickname, it has become irksomely common in recent years to hear the All Blacks referred to as 'the ABs', a cute diminution that implies an assumed familiarity and suggests a lack of respect. Some New Zealand union staff also used the phrase, despite the union spending a considerable amount of money protecting and enforcing the real name. A former union chief executive, David Rutherford, had to remind his staff that the team's name was 'All Blacks' and not 'ABs' or 'the Blacks'.

In Praise of the Haka

Joseph Banks, that inveterate collector of flora and fauna on Captain James Cook's first voyage to New Zealand in 1769–70, found time amid his recording of all the exotica he came across to also write in wonder about the haka.

He talked of protruding tongues and bulging eyes. 'In short nothing is omittd which can render a human shape frightful and deformd which I suppose they think terrible.'

Spelling aside, it's been written about in like manner ever since. Thanks to its use by the All Blacks and by other sports teams — but not all — the haka is one of the most distinctive features of New Zealand in the eyes of the rest of the world. Different countries have different iconography with which they are instantly identified — the Americans, the British and others by their flags, and the French and Welsh by their national anthems. New Zealand has the haka.

Abel Tasman and his crews were evidently the first white men to see a haka. Tasman wrote in his journal that when they neared land, two canoes approached and the men on board 'began to call out to us in a rough, hollow voice, but we could not understand a word of what they said.' Historian Anne Salmond, in her 1991 book, *Two Worlds*, thought the 'rough' calling was probably a haka.

The echoes of those words heard by Tasman's men have been heard around the world ever since. The haka is a key part of Maori culture as an art form and as an expression, but it has gone way beyond that in the eyes of most New Zealanders and the rest of the world to become an integral expression of New Zealand nationalism, especially in sport.

While it is most associated with the All Blacks, it seems to pop up wherever New

Zealanders congregate overseas and often at home. It has become an expression of 'New Zealandness', however bizarre some of its renditions may seem.

The haka became part of the All Blacks' baggage precisely because it was Maori ritual. The first New Zealand team to go to Britain — the New Zealand Native Team of 1888 — were the first sportsmen to take the haka to Britain. The manager of the team, James Scott, a Gisborne publican, said before the team left that the players would perform a haka before each match and would take with them elaborate 'mats' and traditional costume to embellish the performances. Canterbury historian Greg Ryan quoted him as saying that the display would 'no doubt be at once novel and attractive.'

This duly happened. The *Illustrated London News* ran a full page of sketches of the Natives' first match, against Surrey, and one of them was of the players uttering their 'war cry'. The haka seemed to serve the dual purpose of cultural significance and of commercial opportunism. 'This intimidates the other side and attracts huge piles of gate money,' the Sydney *Bulletin* noted.

Frank Marshall, an English cleric who wrote prolifically about rugby, saw the haka as a gimmick whose usefulness was overtaken by the quality of the Natives' rugby. 'In the early matches of the tour,' he wrote, 'the New Zealanders appeared on the field in their native mats and headdresses and uttered their well-known cry of 'Ake, ake, kia kaha' . . . and undoubtedly curiosity had much to do with the attendance at the games. Later, when the real merit of their play was recognised, they discarded these advertising spectacles and depended upon their genuine exhibition of football to attract spectators.'

The *Sporting Life* described the haka as a 'whoop in the vernacular'.

It was the next team in Britain, the Original All Blacks of 1905–06, who introduced the 'Ka Mate!' or Te Rauparaha haka, the one most familiar to New Zealanders. It's commonly supposed that the Originals performed the haka before every match,

How the *Illustrated London News* depicted the Natives against Surrey at Richmond in south London.

but that appears not to be the case. Newspaper reports of the early matches do not mention the haka at all and it's reasonable to assume that because of its novelty they would have. It appears the haka made no pre-match appearance until the fifteenth game, against Blackheath, and the wording of a report in the *Sportsman* supports this supposition: 'The New Zealanders, out of compliments to "The Club", chanted a weirdly interesting Maori haka, to which Blackheath responded by giving three hearty British cheers.' Blackheath had a status in rugby something akin to Marylebone's in cricket.

That does not mean, though, that the All Blacks had not performed the haka until that point. They frequently did so at receptions and 'smoke concerts', usually in response to requests. One of the Originals, Billy Wallace, when writing of a reception put on for the team by the citizens of Newton Abbot in Devon, said: 'At the conclusion of the manager's reply we got on our feet and sang the good old song, "Tenei te tangata pai rawa atu," ["For He's a Jolly Good Fellow"] and wound up with the haka, "Ka Mate! Ka Mate!"'

The Original All Blacks line up on the goal-line before their test against England at Crystal Palace in south London.

Wallace reported that the haka was popular with people in Britain. 'Often when we were asked for our autographs we were also asked to write down the words of our war cry. Most of us could not do so and so [Billy] Stead and [Bill] Cunningham, who were the Maori scholars of the team, wrote it down for us and also a translation. After that we were able to satisfy their curiosity and appear as though we were accomplished Maori linguists.'

The Originals' haka also drew a response when they performed it before the Scottish test. 'No sooner had we finished it than the Australian and New Zealand students in the stand took it up and gave it back at us,' Wallace recalled. The expatriates were medical students at Edinburgh University and included an Otago player, Nolan Fell, who had been picked by Scotland to play against New Zealand. He withdrew because he did not want to play against his compatriots and he was never asked to play for Scotland again.

Into the test section of the tour, the All Blacks did the haka more frequently before matches — prompting various descriptions including 'a weird air' and 'weird invocation'. It also prompted Welsh officials and some players to venture out of Wales to watch the All Blacks in action, the better to work out how to beat them.

Tom Williams, one of their selectors who was a solicitor and a former international, reported back to the Welsh union that the haka was 'very impressive' and suggested the Welsh players should sing the Welsh national anthem after it. This fell on receptive ears, especially after the Cardiff newspaper, the *Western Mail*, translated the haka as imploring the All Blacks to 'be strong and fight to the death'.

The All Blacks — 'these black marionettes,' as the *South Wales Daily News* put it — did the haka in front of a crowd of about 40,000. Welsh rugby historians David Smith and Gareth Williams take up the story: 'Though engulfed in cheers once more the fifteen visitors now had to feel, in their turn, the full effect of the crowd's pent up fervour as the frail melody of "Hen Wlad fy Nhadau" rose up, for the first time, from the players themselves until it was picked up by the multitude and returned from what those on the field seemed "a great wall in mosaic, composed chiefly of flesh-coloured tiles set in sombre-hued cement, splashed with vivid spots of colour".'

The tradition of national anthems before test matches had begun. The fact the anthem followed the haka was to have repercussions a hundred years later.

Whether an expression of culture, pure crowd-pulling entertainment or a ploy by the All Blacks to psyche themselves up for a game at the same time as (hopefully)

intimidating the opposition, the haka from 1905 had become part of the All Blacks. If people overseas watched the All Blacks, they also expected to see a haka — although on most tours it was reserved for test matches only. People at home saw it hardly at all. The haka was not part of the All Blacks' ritual at home games, though they still did it occasionally, and the quality of its delivery generally reflected how infrequently it was done. Haka practice was generally left until the day before the game, amid a great deal of hilarity as choreography and words were hastily learnt.

It was not until the first World Cup in 1987 that the All Blacks brought the haka home for good.

The man who gave the haka more meaning —
Wayne Shelford.

A conscious decision was made by the players to do it properly, to put an end to the embarrassed, self-conscious gestures which had marked the haka for years.

One of the cup players, Wayne Shelford, was responsible for its improved performance. 'There was no pride about the haka at all when I came into the team,' he said. 'I said to Hika Reid, if we are going to do it, we should do it properly. If it isn't done properly, it's an embarrassment to Maoridom.'

Haka practice thereafter became an integral part of the All Blacks' preparation for matches.

The nature of reactions to the haka had changed too. Some opponents saw it as an attempt to give the All Blacks an advantage and wanted no part of it. The Australians, in particular, took to going into a huddle during the haka or idly going through passing drills down at their 22 when it was on. Other opponents stood quietly watching, affecting an air of nonchalance and indifference.

Still others saw it as a challenge to be taken up. When Shelford led the haka against Ireland in Dublin 1989, the Irish lined up arm in arm facing the All Blacks and gradually advanced to within a nose of the New Zealanders. 'I thought it was great,' Shelford said. 'It showed they were not going to back down to us and they played that way too.'

The Irish captain, Willie Anderson, disliked the way the haka gave an advantage to the visiting team but neither did he want to appear disrespectful of it. 'I sat down with coach Jimmy Davidson and we looked at how the haka would get applause for the away team rather than the home team,' Anderson recalled. 'We wanted to turn that psychology around. It wasn't meant to be in any way disrespectful. Then we ended up very close, eyeball to eyeball, and obviously not everyone in the Irish team was totally in line with it. The feeling I had on the day was that you could have cut chunks from the atmosphere.'

Two years later, at the second World Cup, wing Va'aiga Tuigamala broke ranks during the haka before the playoff match against Scotland and advanced, with contrived menace, on Scots John Jeffrey and Tony Stanger. The former Welsh and Lions wing, Gerald Davies, wrote that this turned the haka into a threatening prologue. 'This was gamesmanship,' he said.

When the All Blacks played England in 1997, England hooker Richard Cockerill

All Black flanker Mike Brewer goes high and personal against prop Nick Popplewell before the Ireland test in 1989.

took the haka as a personal challenge and he went toe to toe with his All Black opposite, Norm Hewitt. Cockerill was criticised but his actions were probably more in keeping with ancient Maori response than standing mute or trying to ignore it altogether.

Such gladiatorial confrontations were frowned upon by the International Rugby Board, however, and it instructed match organisers and officials to ensure that a respectable distance was kept between the challengers and the challenged.

As rugby became more and more commercialised and as the amateur days gave way to the professional, the haka became even more a focal point of the All Blacks. The New Zealand Rugby Union's main image for its centennial celebrations in 1992 contained two shots of Steve McDowell in mid-jump at the climax of the haka: one in modern All Black uniform and one in a reproduction of the 1905 gear. (This was despite a Maori view that the jump at the end of the haka should not be part of it).

When adidas took over as the All Blacks' apparel supplier in 1999, it used the haka in some of its promotional material. One mocked-up poster showed a rear view of the Maori prop, Kees Meeuws, performing a haka in front of a lineup of the Original All Blacks.

The frequency of the haka, the increased passion with which the All Blacks performed it and the increasing centrality of it in All Black lore led to all manner of claims and counter-claims. Some Maori deplored it, others applauded it. Some Maori thought the 'Ka Mate!' haka inappropriate and others thought there was nothing wrong with it. The origins of that particular haka were argued over while lawyers were brought in to argue whether the haka was intellectual property and whether the New Zealand union should be charged for its use.

Some All Blacks of earlier eras, who were seldom comfortable whenever they had to perform a haka, felt that it was all going a bit too far. The great Colin Meads, in the direct it-was-different-in-my-day style of his after-dinner speeches, said he thought the All Blacks put more passion into the haka than they did into their rugby. Another former All Black, Chris Laidlaw, thought the haka was being devalued through too-frequent use.

Some current All Blacks did as well and a gathering of players in 1996 considered it was over-used and should be reserved for special occasions. The New Zealand union and match organisers — knowing full well the value of the haka to spectators and television viewers — persuaded the players otherwise.

Maori historian Wira Gardiner, in a book about the haka in 2001, quoted an academic expert on cultural issues, Charles Royal, as saying the rugby union should commission its own haka and thus sidestep claim and counter-claim about who owned what and what it meant.

The All Blacks' manager at the time, Andrew Martin, was quoted as saying there was no intention of having a haka written especially for the All Blacks because they already had one.

But within four years, Royal got his wish. Before the test against South Africa in Dunedin in 2005, the All Blacks lifted the curtain on a brand new haka, one the New Zealand union had commissioned and which some of the players had had a hand in composing.

Written by a Maori scholar, Derek Lardelli, 'Kapo O Pango' was designed to complement rather than replace 'Ka Mate!' In a statement from the New Zealand union, the All Black midfield back, Aaron Mauger, was quoted as saying: 'We felt this group of All Blacks could add to the legacy by writing a haka significant to the All Blacks specifically. "Kapo O Pango" talks about the silver fern, the blackness of the jersey and living your time as an All Black.'

The All Blacks perform 'Kapo o Pango'.

But it wasn't long before it too was surrounded by controversy. Its climax was a throat-slitting gesture — performed most memorably by the Maori halfback, Piri Weepu. Lardelli said it represented the 'cutting edge of sport' and not the slaughter of opponents. Others were not so sure.

Gerald Davies called it a distasteful gesture and said he hoped that haka never saw the light of day again. He thought the nature of the haka — rather than a specific haka — had changed over the years.

'While the haka may once have been appreciated as a celebration of national identity and representing a unique heritage, in recent years it has been transformed into psychological sabre rattling, which the All Blacks clearly think is their right to perform for their advantage as they think fit,' he wrote. 'It was once played facing the crowd in a line; now they defiantly face the players. They should consider that this is a privilege accorded only to them and the other Pacific islanders.'

The haka became the focus again when the All Blacks were in Wales in 2006. The year before, to mark the one-hundredth anniversary of the first test in 1905, the New Zealand team management agreed with a Welsh union request to have the haka precede the Welsh national anthem, as it had done in 1905.

When the All Blacks were back in Cardiff for a test in 2006, the Welsh union said 'Land of My Fathers' would again follow the haka, even though the agreement the previous year had been for that year only. This incensed the All Black management and players and a decision was made not to do the haka at all — at least not publicly.

The players chose instead to do the haka in their dressing room, away from the public gaze, apparently because the haka was primarily for them and not for the public. Despite that, the All Blacks allowed a television crew and photographers into the dressing room.

The All Black captain, Richie McCaw, was quoted in a New Zealand union statement as saying: 'The tradition needs to be honoured properly if we're going to do it. If the other teams want to mess around, we'll just do the haka in the shed . . . haka is about spiritual preparation and we do it for ourselves.' If so, that immediately raised the question of why the dressing room haka was allowed to be filmed and photographed.

In an indication of how far the haka has come, All Black coach Graham Henry was quoted as saying: 'It's about the players really. It's not done for the fans. It's not done for the crowd. It's done for New Zealand rugby and the players themselves.'

83

Whatever the rights and wrongs of the Welsh union and All Black attitudes, it was an episode that reflected well on no one. The Welsh were painted as reneging on an arrangement that had applied the year before, and the All Blacks were accused of petulance and inventing 'tradition' to suit themselves.

The most significant and widely read of British rugby writers, Stephen Jones, was, as usual, cutting in his criticism: 'The All Blacks are labouring under the grossly mistaken impression that their action in performing the haka behind closed doors ... was some kind of heroic gesture. Frankly, I have not come across a single person in British rugby, or a single fan, who did not think that they looked ridiculous.'

Jones, who has been to New Zealand many times, admires the strength and history of All Black rugby but not what he perceives to be the nationalistic arrogance that goes with it. He disagreed that performance of the haka was all about tradition.

'The All Blacks have shattered their own tradition,' he wrote. 'The haka is no longer seen by them, let alone their opponents, as some kind of shining cultural or

Lock Ali Williams in the foreground of the All Blacks' controversial dressing room haka in Cardiff in 2006.

sporting tradition. It is performed as a threat, a pose, an attempt to gain a playing advantage prior to kickoff. The haka is an attempt to get an edge for the match, full stop. Every opposition team has the right to say no, our anthem is last and if you don't like it, don't come.'

There wasn't much that was new in what Jones said. It had all been said before. Australians, more familiar with the haka than any other opponents, tried to dull its edge in 2000 in Sydney when balladeer John Williamson sang 'Waltzing Matilda' after the haka while the Australian players took off their tracksuits. The crowd joined in and it is now the norm for tests in Australia, either with Williamson or some other entertainer leading the crowd. The Australian Rugby Union tried to have it before Wallaby tests in the World Cup in 2003 and although Australia was the host union, the cup company ruled only the haka and other 'traditional' pre-match rituals would be allowed.

The haka in the early years of the twenty-first century has been under the microscope more than any other time since the Natives chanted 'Ake, ake kia kaha' to amused British spectators 120 years ago. While the All Blacks still talk about the tradition of the haka, it has come a long way since it was performed primarily as entertainment for the public.

Grand Slam Finale

The All Blacks have performed the haka in any number of places beyond the rugby ground before a match.

They've done them at dinners and receptions, inside and outside hotels and at airports. But during a match? Even that.

The unprecedented and so far unmatched haka during a game occurred when the All Blacks played the Barbarians in the finale to the grand slam tour of 1978.

It happened about 10 minutes before the end of the game when New Zealand were given a penalty. Halfback Dave Loveridge readied to tap and run but at the same time, captain Graham Mourie gathered a few forwards together and started a haka.

Barbarians players must have been astounded — and a little confused. The haka lasted only a couple of choreographed lines before Loveridge ran and normal transmission was resumed.

Mourie explained it away later as a bit of fun, a bit of enjoyment, at the end of a week in which fun and enjoyment had been in short supply.

The preceding match was the infamous encounter with Bridgend when the Bridgend players seemed to take it upon themselves to save the reputation of Welsh rugby. The All Blacks had not been beaten by a Welsh team and Bridgend were the last hope.

The match was an ill-tempered affair and for all the physical hurts the All Blacks suffered, the most publicity surrounded a gash to the face of Welsh folk hero JPR Williams — a gash said to have been caused by All Black prop John Ashworth.

Williams's father said at the aftermatch function that if he had imagined such incidents might occur, he would never have allowed his sons to play rugby. At that, several of the All Blacks and some of the Bridgend players walked out.

The seamier side of Fleet Street whipped up the outrage against the All Blacks for the rest of the week and the Welsh papers added their bit by pointing out the multinational Barbarians represented the last hope for a victory against the grand slam team on Welsh soil.

Ashworth was booed when he took the field against the Barbarians at halftime and after the game, the New Zealand manager, Russ Thomas, was assaulted by a Welsh fan.

So fun and enjoyment were needed. The in-match haka didn't please the veteran reporter Terry McLean, who was on his last tour for the *New Zealand Herald*. He called it the silliest situation in all of All Black history.

'But a haka?' he wrote. 'Here, on of all places, Cardiff Arms Park? The sight was more than disturbing, it was desolating. Not at any level does one mock the traditions of a great game.' McLean's outrage has to be qualified by the knowledge that one of his brothers co-founded the Barbarians club in Auckland and McLean himself was a proud member of the invitation-only club.

Thomas, as much a British traditionalist as McLean, said he knew Mourie had planned the haka. 'I did not disagree. We felt we had to do something, anything, to lessen the tensions of the Bridgend business.'

And haka or no, the All Blacks still won — though only with a last-minute dropped goal by Eddie Dunn.

Variations on a Theme

The All Blacks have not always performed 'Ka Mate!', the haka with which they have been most associated. One of the most celebrated teams, the 1924-25 Invincibles who toured Britain, France and North America without a loss, had a haka written specially for them — decades before the All Blacks of 2005 had 'Kapo O Pango' written for them.

The Invincibles' haka was witten by a Gisborne man, Wiremu Rangi, and evidently reworked by Frank Acheson, a noted expert on Maori land tenure and a judge of the Native Land Court. Acheson was one of 11 New Zealanders who travelled with the team to Britain and who were described as 'the official party', though they seemed to be a mixture of reporters and supporters.

The Rangi-Acheson haka went:

First part		translated as
Leader:	Kai whaka ngawari au ia hau.	Let us prepare ourselves for the fray.
Team:	I . . . au . . . e . . . hei.	We are ready.
Leader:	Ko niu tire ne haruru nei.	The New Zealand storm is about to break.
Team:	Au . . . au . . . aue . . . ha . . . hei.	The sound of the breaking.
Leader:	Ko niu tireni haruru nei.	The New Zealand storm waxes fiercer.
Team:	Au . . . au . . . aue . . . ha . . . hei.	The height of the storm.
Leader:	A-haha.	Now then!
Team:	Katu te ihi i hi	We shall stand as children of the sun
	Katu te wanawana	We shall climb to the heavens in exaltation of spirit
	Kirunga te rangi.	We shall attain the zenith
	E tu iho nei.	The power! The power!
	Au! Au! Au!	

Second part

		translated as
Leader:	Tena ipoia . . . o rongo Ingarangi hauana te ao e.	Remain alert. The strength of England is known throughout the world.
Team:	A-haha.	Now then!
	Hora hia mai a mahi kia hau.	Let us see what England can do.
	Hora hia mai o tiima kia hau.	Bring forth your strong teams.
	Omahi aku mahi me hui!	Let us combine in friendly rivalry.
Leader:	Nga mahi tinihanga me kiki.	Anything unsportsmanlike together we shall kick aside.
Team:	Au . . . au . . . hei,	The strength of the kick.
Leader:	A-haha.	Now then!
Team:	Ma mutu nga mahi haramai ki tireni.	After our battles are over, come to New Zealand.
	Au! Au! Aue! Ha.	It is ended!

George Nepia leads the Invincible All Blacks in their specially written haka.

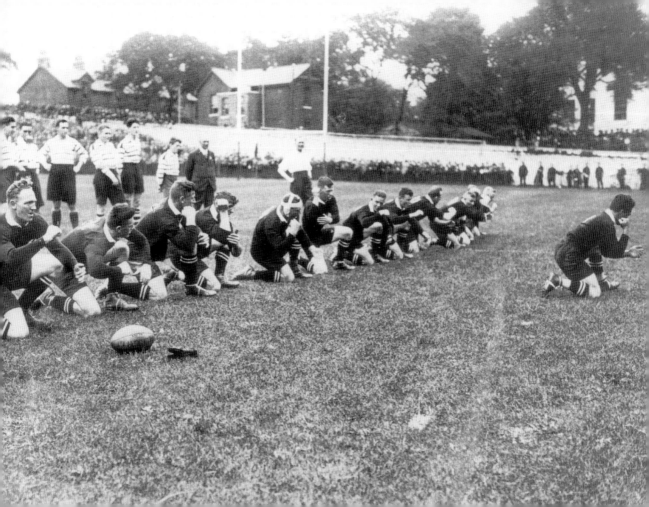

The haka most associated with the All Blacks, 'Ka Mate!' apparently originated with a warrior chief hiding from his enemies beneath a woman.

There are different interpretations, but what seems to be the most widely accepted was that the Ngati Toa chief, Te Rauparaha, wrote the haka in 1821 after a close shave.

According to Sir John Grace in his book, *Tuwharetoa*, Te Rauparaha fled the Ngati Te Aho after attacking them at the base of Mt Tongariro. The Tuwharetoa chief, Te Heu Heu, sent him to Rotoaira chief, Te Wharerangi, for protection.

Te Wharerangi hid Te Rauparaha in a kumara pit and had his wife sit over the entrance. She provided a visual barrier and her genitals were supposed to neutralise the searching incantations of Te Rauparaha's pursuers.

The opening lines are a commentary. Te Rauparaha mutters 'It is death!' when the pursuing chief, Tauteka, arrives. When Te Wharerangi tells Tauteka that his quarry has left, Te Rauparaha says, 'It is life!' When Tauteka expresses doubts, Te Rauparaha is gloomy again: 'It is death!' Then, when Tauteka leaves, Te Rauparaha is a relieved man: 'It is life!'

Its use has made 'Ka Mate!' a national haka, though it does not find total favour in the South Island where the dominant iwi is Ngai Tahu, who suffered at Te Rauparaha's hands.

The words and a common translation in English (other translations differ in content if not in form):

Maori	translated as
Ka mate! Ka mate!	It is death! It is death!
Ka ora! Ka ora!	It is life! It is life!
Ka mate! Ka mate!	It is death! It is death!
Ka ora! Ka ora!	It is life! It is life!
Tenai te tangata puhuruhuru	Behold. There stands the hairy man
Nana nei te tiki mai!	Coming into . . .
I whakawhiti te ra!	The light of the sun
Upane! Upane!	One step forward
Upane! Ka upane!	Another upward step
Whiti te ra!	Into the sun!

The earliest recording of the 'Ka mate! Ka mate!' haka may date from the Original All Blacks' tour of the northern hemisphere in 1905–06 when the technology of recording sound was still in its infancy.

Thomas Edison developed his phonograph in 1877. Within 10 years, sounds could be recorded on wax cylinders and the first gramophone records were produced in the United States in 1892.

Two of the Original All Blacks, Billy Wallace and Freddy Roberts, went to visit some of Roberts's relatives in Newcastle at the end of the British section of the tour in late January, 1906.

'On the Sunday night, after we had returned from church, we had a little party and we got the gramophone going,' Wallace wrote. 'The chap had a little gadget for making records and he got Fred and I to do the haka and the chorus of "Tenei te tangata pai rawa atu," ["For He's a Jolly Good Fellow"] while an impression was made on a wax cylinder. Then we were able to hear it reproduced on the gramophone.

The haka was not always well choreographed and rehearsed. This one is at Athletic Park in Wellington in 1923.

'But soon afterwards one of the youngsters knocked the record off the table and broke it. Fortunately, he had another record left so we had to repeat the performance.'

The All Blacks made another technological breakthrough on their tour. Their test against England at Crystal Palace in south London was the first international rugby match to be recorded on film, a copy of which is preserved at the New Zealand Film Archive.

* * * *

The international renown of the All Blacks' haka was the platform for an elaborate, but unsuccessful, hoax early in 2007.

Some unidentified person or people prepared a 'press release' purporting to originate from the International Rugby Board saying that as a result of complaints to the IRB about the haka, other countries would now be permitted to mount their own pre-match displays.

The 'release' looked the part: it carried the logos of the IRB and the 2007 World Cup and was written in the name of the IRB chairman, Syd Millar. One giveaway to its falseness was that Millar's name was misspelt 'Miller'.

Its content, however, proved it was a hoax. Something so elaborate or imaginative could hardly be attributed to the IRB.

Among the pre-match displays approved, it said, were:

- The England team will chat about the weather, wave hankies in the air and attach bells to their ankles before moaning about how they invented the game and gave it to the world, but no one appreciates them.
- The Ireland team will split into two, with the southern half performing a 'Riverdance', while the northerners march the traditional route from their dressing room to the pitch, via their opponents' dressing room.
- The Americans will not attend until almost fulltime. In future years they will amend the records to show that they were in fact the most important team in the tournament and Hollywood will make a blockbuster film called 'Saving Flanker Ryan'.
- Five of the Canadian team will sing 'La Marsellaise' and hold the rest of the team to ransom.
- The Australians will have a barbecue on their side of the field and invite the opposition over before the game. The food and alcohol will be in abundance and by the start of the game no one will remember what they came to the stadium for. After some streaking, the singing of dirty songs and the occasional chunder, everyone will go home thoroughly convinced it was a bloody good night.

Boks, Wallabies Follow

Just as Australia and South Africa followed New Zealand with nicknames for their national rugby teams (the Wallabies in 1908 and the Springboks in 1906), they also attempted to follow the Original All Blacks with a 'haka' of their own.

The difference was the New Zealanders did the haka because they wanted to; the others had their versions of it foisted upon them by people who still had, in Edwardian times, a 'noble savagery' view of the colonies and were anxious to see the quaint customs of the natives. The view seemed to be that, if the All Blacks had their haka, then the others would also have their native chants, whether they liked it or not.

Another, more significant difference was that the All Blacks included Maori while the Springboks of 1906 and the Wallabies of 1908 were entirely of European ethnic origin and would remain so for many years. The South Africans, who toured Britain for the first time a year after the Originals, adopted a Zulu 'war cry', or so it was described, and the Australians had to suffer the indignity of performing a supposed Aboriginal greeting.

The Springboks performed their so-called war cry before each match, as vice-captain Paddy Carolin recorded in his diary of the tour. 'We drove to the ground in brakes, had our photos taken, gave our war cry and then played our first game,' he wrote after the opening match against East Midlands in Northampton.

The South Africans' chant went like this:

> Ghee gammilio gashee
> Ghee gammilio gashee
> Gee ghammilio gashee
> Wha!

Players in the original Australian team two years later were handed printed copies of their chant when they boarded their ship in Sydney for the voyage to Britain. It was called 'The Native Greeting to Strangers in Peace' and was said to have been authenticated by the Royal Geographic Society. An Australian sports historian, Peter Sharpham, wrote that the war cry was in fact borrowed word for word from the Newtown Rugby Football Club's war cry, which was printed in Newtown match programmes and annual reports at the time.

It went like this:

	translated as
Gau Gau [opponent's name] Whir-r-r	Greetings to _____ in (place)
Win-nang-a lang (Thur)	You are great men
Mu-e-an-yil-ling	We are pleased to meet you
Bu rang-a-lang (Yang)	We think we can beat you
Yai! Yai! Gun-yil-lang yang yah!	Come, let us try

New South Wales (in the days when there was no Australian team) performs its 'corroboree' in Wellington.

The words handed to the players were accompanied by instructions:

1. Slapping the thighs three times to begin together.
2. Putting left foot forward and throwing out left hand, holding right by side.
3. Hands at breast and at the word 'Gau' hands to be stretched palms down.
4. Hands up at full extent.
5. Hands in front at full extent and at the word 'Gang' dropped to the left with force.
6. Left hand at full extent raised from front to right rear over shoulder finishing at the word 'yah', facing your right then from a stooping attitude one long sustained 'Coo-ee' while making a complete circle from left to right.

The team performed it on the deck of the ship on arrival at Plymouth, before each match and at various social functions during the tour.

For all its apparent success among British crowds, it did not impress the Wallabies' captain, Paddy Moran.

He wrote his autobiography in 1939 and said: 'The memory of that war cry provokes anger in me even after all these years.' He related how New Zealand teams 'performed some antics' before a match because it was the Maori tradition to 'lash themselves into some sort of fury by this picturesque method of self-suggestion.' Any such chants adopted by Australian teams were merely for comic relief, he wrote. 'Now we were being asked to remind British people of the miserable remnants of a race which they had dispossessed and we had maltreated or neglected.'

Moran, a well-educated and normally mild mannered man who became a pioneer in cancer research, gave full vent to his disgust at what he described as foolish and a pantomime:

'I refused to lead the wretched caricature of a native corroboree and regularly hid myself among the team, a conscientious objector. None of the men liked it. The average Australian has a keen sense of the ridiculous and dislikes acting in a burlesque or wearing any strange regalia. The final argument used by the Rugby Union was that it had a box office value. The people in England expected it, they said. They might just as reasonably have expected us to wear the broad arrow on our left arms as a respectful tribute to our first families. As it was, we performed shamefacedly some grotesque antics before crowds that were patently not interested in the indifferent show. They and we had come to the ground for an entirely different purpose, so as soon as the business was over some of us rushed to hide our heads in the first available scrum.'

Ridiculous it may have been and geared solely toward British audiences as it was, the Australians nevertheless offered a reprise 16 years later at the Sydney Cricket Ground before a match against New Zealand. There was no Australian team for most of the 1920s, so 'Gau Gau' etc. came from entirely New South Wales throats. It may have had some effect because New South Wales won.

All 'Blacks Arts'

New Zealanders dabbled in the black arts but lost both the music and the rugby when the Original All Blacks first played Wales in 1905 — or so said a Welsh newspaper columnist.

'Ariel', writing in the *Evening Express,* had plenty to say about the historic match when the haka was followed by an impromptu rendition of *Land of My Fathers*, thus beginning the tradition of national anthems before test matches.

'There has been a prevailing impression that the New Zealanders have been dealing with the black art whilst touring in England and that it commences with their war dance,' he wrote. 'I began to feel this keenly, and directly they had opened the concert we replied with our innocent patriotic air. The Maori song was a weird incantation, with a diabolical intent to do harm to somebody. Ours was mere sentimental piffle about the land of our fathers.'

'Ariel' thought the words of the haka looked innocent gibberish in Maori 'but

I knew they were playing simply on our ingenuous natures and it bears the same relation to forthcoming events as the witches' incantation in "Macbeth". It's flat dealing with the devil!'

He was not impressed with the musical qualities of the haka. 'The tenors were very much out of it and the basses were quite a tone too low — lower than the guttural welcome given by aborigines to intrepid explorers of long ago.'

'Ariel' talked about a man near him in the stand who was incensed at the cheek of 'the Maoris' in bringing such music to Wales — the land of song and of the eisteddfod. 'It made his blood boil, he said. They may teach us football, said he, but it's going a bit too far to bring such music as that to palm off such trashy psalmody on an enlightened musical people.

'But our men [the Welsh players] were not much better in their "Hen Wlad fy Nhadau." They pitched it decidedly low and could not be heard, but the crowd soon took it up and then it boomed. The Zealanders seemed to consider this an innovation and scarcely tolerable, but they had to stand still and listen to Welsh music for once. Then both sides faced the real music.'

Trans-Tasman Trophy

On the Bledisloe Cup, that most prized trophy for competition between New Zealand and Australia, there is a little shield pinned to the base that says New Zealand won the cup for the first time in 1931.

Unassailable proof, anyone could be forgiven for thinking, that the cup matches began in that year. But they did not.

New Zealand and Australia certainly played each other on 12 September 1931, at Eden Park, and the All Blacks won 20–13. But they did not play for the Bledisloe Cup. They could not have. The cup did not exist until the following year.

The minutes of the New Zealand Rugby Football Union's management committee record that at a meeting on 23 September — 11 days after the test — the chairman, Stan Dean, told the meeting the Governor-General, Lord Bledisloe, wanted to present a trophy for inter-Anzac rugby.

'After consultation with the New South Wales union,' the minutes say, 'the offer was accepted . . . a letter be sent to the Governor-General thanking him for his generous donation and informing him that the trophy, which will be known as the Bledisloe Cup, will be played for in test matches between the two countries.'

In June of 1932 the New Zealand Press Association circulated a story originating from Auckland that the cup had arrived from England. The story gave the dimensions of the cup, described what was inscribed on it, and recorded it had been designed by Nelson Isaac, the head of the art school at Wellington Technical College, and was made by silversmiths Walker and Hall in London.

It then said: 'The announcement of the presentation of the cup was made last September. The first game of the first series of matches for it will be played in Sydney on Saturday.'

The Wallabies won that first test 22–17, but the All Blacks won the second in

Brisbane 21–3 and the decider in Sydney 21–13, thus becoming the first holders of the Bledisloe Cup.

The All Blacks had the cup with them anyway. They took it to Australia and put it on the touchline for each of the tests, but they didn't take formal possession of it until the Friday after the third test, at a farewell function at the Hotel Wentworth in Sydney.

So how come the cup has a shield on its base saying it was won by New Zealand in 1931? It has to be assumed that since Bledisloe's offer was made and accepted that year, someone at the New Zealand union decided to award it in retrospect.

It's only in the last 30 or so years that the cup has acquired something of the status of the holy grail for All Blacks and Wallabies, and a sports marketer's dream. For much of its

What Anzac rugby supremacy is all about: the Bledisloe Cup.

history, it was won so often by New Zealand that it seemed to be permanently nailed down on a shelf above the landing on the stairs within the union's offices in the Huddart Parker Building in central Wellington. It even spent a period when no one quite knew where it was. A New Zealand journalist who covered the 1951 All Blacks' tour of Australia, Bruce Hewitt, said the cup went missing for a while and was eventually traced to a dusty storeroom in Melbourne. It had been borrowed for a tourism promotion and forgotten, eventually to be rediscovered among cardboard trees and sheep.

It was only with the resurgence of Australian rugby in the late 1970s that the cup became a celebrated prize.

Bledisloe was an active donor in 1931. Apart from the cup for rugby, among his other gifts were a new Black Rod to Parliament, a challenge trophy for cultivating native plants, a 'loving cup' for guides and rangers, a Lord Bledisloe Medal for oratory and a silver cup for the New Zealand women's tennis champion.

The Silver Fern

The Silver Fern has always been a distinctive part of the New Zealand rugby uniform.

It first appeared on the jerseys of the New Zealand Natives team that toured Britain and Australia in 1888–89 and was adopted by the New Zealand Rugby Football Union in its second year of existence in 1893.

The Silver Fern, along with the kiwi, is one of the most instantly recognisable symbols of New Zealand overseas.

The fern now appears in stylised versions for copyright and trademark purposes, but the original was modelled on the distinctive *Cyathea dealbata*, a fern frond with a silver underside. It is found from North Cape to Dunedin, but largely absent from the West Coast and the south of the South Island.

One theory for the fern being adopted as a national sporting emblem was that Maori regarded the fern root as a food suitable for warriors and others engaged in arduous pursuits, as opposed to the kumara, which represented peace and fertility.

In Maori mythology, the parent of the fern root

One of the Originals' jerseys worn by George Nicholson.

is generally Haumia. The Arawa people regarded him as one of the sons of Rangi and Papa, the first parents. In parts of the North Island, Haumia is a son of Tane and grandson of Rangi and Papa.

The kiwi only came to be widely associated with New Zealand toward the end of World War I when a concert party for troops was named the Kiwis, which also used a silver fern emblem. (Another was called the Tuis). The first and most enduring association in sport for the kiwi was with the national league team, though the Second New Zealand Expeditionary Force rugby team after World War II also became known as the Kiwis.

The modern version of the All Black jersey.

All Black Statistics

Statistics accurate to 31 August 2007

All Black tests							
	Played	Won	Drawn	Lost	For	Against	% (of wins)
Argentina	13	12	1	-	585	180	92.3
Australia	128	85	5	38	2395	1656	70.8
Britain (Lions, Anglo-Welsh etc)	38	29	3	6	634	345	76.3
Canada	3	3	-	-	170	26	100
England	29	22	1	6	652	364	75.8
Fiji	4	4	-	-	304	36	100
France	45	34	1	10	1104	579	75
Ireland	20	19	1	-	517	199	95
Italy	8	8	-	-	521	82	100
Japan	1	1	-	-	145	17	100
Pacific Islands	1	1	-	-	41	26	100
Romania	1	1	-	-	14	6	100
Scotland	25	23	2	-	704	285	92
South Africa	72	40	3	29	1289	1081	55.5
Tonga	3	3	-	-	238	16	100
United States	2	2	-	-	97	9	100
Wales	23	20	-	3	693	216	86.9
Samoa	4	4	-	-	207	42	100
World XV	3	2	-	1	94	69	66.6
	424	314	17	93	10,468	5247	73.8

All Black Top Fives

Most games for New Zealand

Colin Meads

133 Colin Meads (1957–71)
128 Sean Fitzpatrick (1986–97)
117 Andy Haden (1972–85)
113 Ian Kirkpatrick (1967–77)
113 Bryan Williams (1970–78)

Most tests

Sean Fitzpatrick

92 Sean Fitzpatrick (1986–97)
81 Justin Marshall (1995–2005)
79 Ian Jones (1990–99)
74 Tana Umaga (1997–2005)
70 Andrew Mehrtens (1995–2004)

Most points in all matches

1067 Grant Fox (1984–93)
994 Andrew Mehrtens (1995–2004)
781 Don Clarke (1956–64)
636 Dan Carter (2003–)
453 Fergie McCormick (1965–71)

Grant Fox

Most points in tests

967 Andrew Mehrtens (1995–2004)
645 Grant Fox (1984–93)
636 Dan Carter (2003–)
291 Carlos Spencer (1997–2004)
236 Christian Cullen (1996–2002)

Andrew Mehrtens

Most tries in all matches

67 John Kirwan (1984–94)
65 Bryan Williams (1970–78)
52 Christian Cullen (1996–2002)
50 Ian Kirkpatrick, Jeff Wilson (1993–2001), Stu Wilson (1976–83)
48 Terry Wright (1986–92)

John Kirwan

Most tries in tests

46	Christian Cullen (1996–2002)
44	Jeff Wilson (1993–2001)
43	Doug Howlett (2000–)
38	Joe Rokocoko (2003–)
37	Jonah Lomu (1994–2002)

Christian Cullen

Most tests as captain

51	Sean Fitzpatrick (1992–97)
30	Wilson Whineray (1958–65)
22	Taine Randell (1998-2002), Reuben Thorne (2002–03)
21	Tana Umaga (2004–05)
20	Graham Mourie (1977–82), Richie McCaw (2004–)

Sean Fitzpatrick